"There is no denyin[g] ___ tion, and lack of m___ Jeremy Linneman h___ ___ into the root causes and, better still, a cure. If you are among the many who have been wounded by the church or have abandoned it altogether because you never felt genuinely connected, this short book is for you. It may well prove to be your first step back into the spiritual life of the body of Christ, the only place where meaningful community can be found."

Sam Storms, Founder and President, Enjoying God Ministries

"This is like a heartfelt devotional with a call to respond. Jeremy Linneman gives us researched help for understanding why we're often so lonely. Then he suggests practical steps for the hard but rewarding work of community building. Embedded with rich theology and the sure promises of God, these pages challenge us to practice and experience how we belong to God and to each other."

Tasha Chapman, Professor of Educational Ministries, Covenant Theological Seminary; coauthor, *The Politics of Ministry* and *Resilient Ministry*

"From the first paragraph, Jeremy Linneman had me engaged in this important but overlooked topic. Reading on, I was encouraged by his insightful proposals to address the loneliness that is all too pervasive in the church. You will want not only to read this thoughtful work but also to employ its practical suggestions to develop and experience true belonging in your life and church."

Nora Allison, former women's ministry director; Retreat Speaker, Seminary Wives Institute

Why Do We Feel Lonely at Church?

TGC Hard Questions

Jared Kennedy, Series Editor

Why Do We Feel
Lonely at Church?

Jeremy Linneman

CROSSWAY®

WHEATON, ILLINOIS

Why Do We Feel Lonely at Church?

Copyright © 2023 by Jeremy Linneman

Published by Crossway
   1300 Crescent Street
   Wheaton, Illinois 60187

Portions of this booklet build on the author's online article "How Your Church Can Respond to the Loneliness Epidemic," TGC, August 14, 2018, https://www.thegospelcoalition.org/.

Cover design: Ben Stafford

Cover images: Unsplash

First printing 2023

Printed in the United States of America

Trade paperback ISBN: 978-1-4335-9169-3
ePub ISBN: 978-1-4335-9171-6
PDF ISBN: 978-1-4335-9170-9

Library of Congress Control Number: 2023939546

Crossway is a publishing ministry of Good News Publishers.

BP			32	31	30	29	28	27	26	25	24	23
15	14	13	12	11	10	9	8	7	6	5	4	3	2	1

Contents

NOT LONG AGO, I SAT WITH A FRIEND as she described why she struggles with trusting the church anymore. She's not leaving, but she feels hurt and is increasingly disconnected. A few months earlier, I talked with a couple who have attended our church sporadically for a few years. They liked it, they said, but they have so many issues with "the church" that they just need a break from it. Another friend still considers herself a believer but hasn't attended church in several years and doesn't plan to return anytime soon. I can think of countless other stories, and I'm guessing you can too.

The church in North America has been in decline for decades. Many researchers and organizations give two reasons. First, Christian beliefs have become increasingly unpopular in our secular culture. So, many churchgoers have dropped certain convictions or stopped attending altogether in order to maintain relationships outside the church. Second, the church's moral reputation has been brought into question, as key leaders and political figures have claimed Christianity yet lived opposite to its teachings.

Although I'm sure these two reasons are important factors, I think there's a different reason why many people are "deconstructing," "deconverting," or just simply leaving the church.

I believe the problem is *a lack of belonging*.

People don't feel connected, known, or loved. So they leave.

My observations as a pastor drawing on my experience are, at best, anecdotal. But I have spoken with many pastors and believers who agree that belonging is the leading issue in the church. People reject Christianity not primarily because of our doctrine but because of our lack of intentionality in relationships. They're leaving the church not mainly because of the failures of public figures but because their Christian neighbors aren't loving. And while we should be concerned if people are leaving for any reason, we should be crushed that people are leaving for this one. I'm convinced that what the church most needs right now is deep, loving, Christ-shaped community.

Throughout this book, when I talk about *church*, I'm referring to the local church: a group of believers under the shepherding of its pastors and leaders, gathering for worship and (most likely) in smaller groups. When I talk about *community*, I mean the shared life of those church members: the hospitality, discipleship, prayer, ministry, and service that happens between believers and overflows to those outside the church.

———

Over the last six years, I've studied loneliness, belonging, and community, and I'm convinced we don't fully understand the pervasiveness of individualism—and how much it is hurting us as believers. How did social isolation become such a trend? To what extent do Christians experience loneliness? And how can the church respond to the loneliness epidemic?

These questions matter immensely to me, and not just as an intellectual exercise. I've been in pastoral ministry for more than fifteen years, and for the last five years, I have pastored a young congregation that is the most loving, relationally intimate group of people I have ever experienced. And yet, even here we're constantly feeling the effects of radical individualism, and our own community

3

is far from perfect. (No church on this side of the new creation will be perfect.) This book is not mere theory; it's one pastor's heartfelt attempt to serve the church by calling it back to its relational roots.

I have three readers in mind. The first is the struggling Christian I already mentioned. She's been wondering if anyone really cares about her; perhaps she's been away from church for a while, and no one has called. "Why do I feel lonely at church?" she might well be asking.

The second reader is a pastor whose church is full of lonely people, yet they're resisting further involvement in small groups and community ministries. Worse yet, they don't even realize they're lonely; they just feel overwhelmed and busy. He wants to know how to encourage his members to create a community that reflects the church of the New Testament.

The third reader is between the first two. She's invested in her local church and serves in small group leadership. She resonates with the concerns and disconnection of the first reader and knows her pastor is facing all the challenges of the second reader. She's looking to understand our epidemic of loneliness, find hope for her small group, and equip those she serves.

I hope this book helps you face the hard questions many believers are afraid to consider. I hope it gives you a deep foundation: We are relational beings, we were created for community, and the church is designed to be a place of true belonging. I hope this book gives you a sense of hope, optimism, and courage as you engage your own community. I hope it helps you discover your place of true belonging—that you can be fully known and fully loved in Christ and his beautiful church. And, most of all, my prayer is that it serves to lift your eyes to Christ, for the sake of his glory and your own formation in him.

Epidemic of Loneliness

Early in my first pastoral position, I was invited to dinner by a family in our church. They talked at length about their marriage and children but said nothing of church community and friendship. I asked a question I had never asked in that context before: "Do you have any friends?"

"Ah," the husband said, looking at his wife. "No, we don't really have any friends." They explained the schedule of two working adults with two children in private schools with additional sports involvement. They said they had friends when they met each other, but in the two decades of marriage that followed, they hadn't maintained a single friendship. They seemed to shrug this off and smile. I can remember my surprise more than twelve years later: How could Christians be friendless? And just how common is this?

As I've continued in my pastoral ministry, I've met and ministered among countless people like this. They don't feel lonely, but they do feel busy, overwhelmed, and fragmented. They want friends but have embraced a lifestyle that makes friendship and community almost impossible. They go to church, attend a small group, pray, and read their Bibles. But their understanding of relationships and community has been far more conditioned by the radical individualism of our society than by the biblical foundation. As a result, deep relationships—beyond marriage and family—seem like an optional add-on to life.

Epidemic of the Twenty-First Century

Americans are lonelier than ever. Even with affordable phone calls and free email, we are talking to one another less. Despite the high prevalence of car ownership and the low cost of cross-country air travel, we are spending less time with our families.[1]

Research demonstrates that loneliness causes "an insidious type of stress" that leads to chronic inflammation and an increased risk of heart disease, arthritis, and diabetes.[2] In fact, loneliness has the same effect on mortality as smoking fifteen cigarettes a day.[3] Loneliness may be *the* epidemic of contemporary Western culture. Most of our other epidemics—from heart disease to pornography use—can trace their roots back to a lonely heart.

Social scientists have been aware of these trends for years. In 2001, Harvard researcher Robert Putnam published an influential book, *Bowling Alone*.[4] He demonstrated that American social trends can be summarized with a simple illustration: While bowling leagues are in decline, more people are bowling than ever. Why? People are bowling alone. In the past two decades, this individualistic trend has not only continued; it's been supercharged. In our new generation of social media, online shopping, and remote work, people aren't just bowling alone. We're scrolling alone.

And this is true not merely of nonreligious people. Church members, too, are increasingly isolated from their neighbors and from fellow believers.

How did we get to this point?

Vanishing Relationships

Loneliness is the unsurprising symptom of an individualistic society. Sociologist Marc Dunkelman has made the case that unexpected encounters in our local communities are key to a sense of belonging. In public spaces like grocery stores, coffee shops, and playgrounds, neighbors connect through healthy discussion face-to-face. But these days, these localized conversations have been replaced by frantic tapping on small glowing screens separated by hundreds of miles. Dunkelman suggests this shift reflects the larger problem of vanishing American community.

> Adults today tend to prize different kinds of connections than their grandparents: more of our time and attention today is spent on more intimate contacts and the most casual acquaintances. We've abandoned the relationships in between . . . "middle-ring" ties.[5]

Dunkelman's research shows that Americans' closest relationships, the "inner-ring" connections of marriage, children, and parents, have not significantly changed over the past half century. And we still have many "outer-ring" ties, those neighbors, coworkers, and drive-thru employees with whom we interact only in small, nonmeaningful pieces. But the frequency and quality of these middling-ring relationships—with friends, church members, close neighbors, coworkers, and fellow students—have been drastically reduced. Without these middle-ring ties, our social fabric begins to disintegrate. When front porches are replaced by back decks, it limits our interactions with our neighbors. When college students choose virtual classrooms, it means far less community at a formative stage of life. When church members watch services from home, it hinders spiritual growth and diminishes the potential for the church to cultivate meaningful community.

We are social beings, and human connection is essential for our brain functioning, physical health, and emotional well-being. We are hardwired to connect, and yet modern American society has severely diminished the frequency of our interactions and the quality of our relationships.

And Then, COVID Happened

Prior to COVID-19, the epidemic of loneliness was in full swing. *And then we were all locked in our homes indefinitely.*

During the pandemic year, the average American's daily time spent with people outside his or her household dropped by a full hour. Over eight months, this amounts to about 244 fewer hours spent in relationships in 2020 versus 2019.[6]

The pandemic saw increases in our texting, phone calls, video conferencing, TV streaming, computer use, and video game use. Not including work and school time, the average American increased daily screen time by about sixty minutes. When we put these two trends together, we discover this: in 2020, the average American traded three hundred hours of in-person time with friends, church members, and neighbors for three hundred hours of social media, TV, and Internet reading.

But it's not just that in-person relationships have been replaced with screen time. The types of relationships we maintain have radically changed as well.

Fewer and More Divisive Relationships

Without the common grace of good friends, we can get lost in a web of so-called friendships (what David French calls "factional friendships") that are based on social-political alignment and little else.[7] Unless we have a healthy network of family, friends, and church—based on something more significant than identical social and political views—then these faction friendships can damage individuals, churches, and society. And without a proper view of God's purposes for our lives together, we'll see church as just another optional social gathering.

Further, social media has sorted us into tiny homogenous cliques. Though it began around the promise of increased connection in a transient culture, social media has instead driven us to connect with people *like us*—and likely an exaggerated form of ourselves. As a result, social media has become the ideal platform for rewarding extreme views and muting moderate ones. It's not a great place to present our views, receive alternative views, and engage in civil discourse. Instead, it's just one more way to identify yourself with certain groups (and *not* others) and establish a personal brand.[8] Our experience over the last few years suggests a distinction: there's *passive loneliness* (lacking friends and community) and *divisive loneliness* (rejecting friends and community unless they are in total agreement with one's social, political, and religious views). Said another way, there can be a dark side to belonging.

Unless we can restore our opportunities for shared, generous conversation between two very different people, we'll have little hope for our shared social life seeing any improvement. Just think of the importance for the local church. Our union with Christ means profound, supernatural unity with one another, yet everything in our culture challenges this fellowship.

Why It's So Hard to Have Friends at Church

These shifts even affect us in the church. Our unity in Christ—so wonderfully important across the New Testament—is being threatened by a number of social forces. Reaching depth in our relationships is harder than ever. Cultivating a thriving community in each church has never been more difficult.

Every now and then, I'll be talking with a newer member at Trinity Community Church, Columbia, Missouri, and he or she will express disappointment that after several months he or she has only a few friendships. "That's a great start," I respond. "It will take a while!"

First, we are isolated from the relationships we most need; we have fewer social interactions and less relational connection than previous generations of believers. Second, we are lonelier than we realize; we likely don't appreciate how much of our spiritual and emotional well-being has been disrupted by loneliness. Third, we feel busy, overwhelmed, and disconnected; we desperately need relationships but may feel too busy to take the time to form real relationships with others in the church. Fourth, it's harder than it should be to form meaningful friendships and middle-ring relationships; many of our peers at church are struggling with a misunderstood loneliness as well. If I'm talking to a leader, I will add a fifth: each church is full of lonely people, and we need to be far more intentional about how we cultivate community.

If you are finding it hard to make friends, you're not crazy. Friendship is challenging in a society like this—even in the church. But the answer is not to lower your expectations and prepare for loneliness. The answer is to confront the challenge directly, reject the isolation and division of our times, and embrace real, meaningful, face-to-face relationships with imperfect people. By God's grace and intentional steps, we can do this.

The Search for True Belonging

"You belong here."

We find these words on the walls of fitness clubs, in social media groups, and throughout coworking spaces. From psychologists and therapists to retail store advertisers, everywhere we turn are promises of belonging. Why has this need become a trending topic and marketing hook in our culture? We're busy, lonely, and overwhelmed. Building and keeping relationships is much harder than it should be.

How can we find a place to belong in a culture like ours? What, if anything, does Scripture have to say about belonging? And how might Christian believers and churches cultivate places of belonging?

Belonging is a core human need. Beyond food and shelter, nothing promotes human flourishing like having a people and a place. Research confirms that income level, marriage and children, and perceived security all pale in comparison to belonging for promoting sustained happiness in one's life.[9] We long to belong.

And we need a belonging deeper than what the world can offer. True belonging means being fully known and fully loved by God and one another.

About seven years ago, I had lunch with a church member, and he mentioned that his previous graduate research (in education theory) was focused on belonging. I admitted I had no idea what that meant. He explained that throughout the twentieth century, the reigning psychological hypothesis stated that individuals were most fully satisfied when they had a high sense of self-esteem—that is, when individuals believed in and thought highly of themselves. But later research came to a startling conclusion: self-esteem had little to no positive effect on individuals' lives, and for many it had negative effect.

That led researchers to ask, If not self-esteem, then what single quality was most identified with satisfaction and well-being? In 1995, social psychologist Roy Baumeister published a substantial article that demonstrated that the healthiest, most satisfied individuals in life are those who have *a place to belong*.[10] In other words, our deepest satisfaction comes, not from achieving personal autonomy but through acceptance into unconditional love and an unbreakable connection to a people.

As Christians, we don't find this surprising. The Bible shows us that we have been created in the image of a relational God, that belonging is a significant blessing of life in the family of God, and that even our best human relationships serve to remind us of our ultimate relationship—communion with God.

Belonging in Scripture

Belonging has deep roots in the biblical story and Christian theology: we belong to God and his family through the life, death, and resurrection of Jesus.

The Bible invites us into something far deeper than mere religious belief. God's grand story shows us that he created us to know him, worship him, and dwell with him forever. Yet our sin severed this relationship. In the garden of Eden, Adam and Eve's sin caused a break in the most beautiful relationship, and they were removed from God's immediate presence. But even then, a promise was given: *You are my people, and I will bring you back to myself* (see Gen. 3:1–24).

Many years later, God spoke to Abraham and promised to make him a great people. Though he had no children and no idea where God was leading him, God made another promise: *You will be my people, and I will be your God* (see Gen. 12:1–3 and 15:1–6).

Still later, God's beloved people were enslaved in Egypt to a brutal oppressor. Again, God spoke a promise of blessing: *I am your God, and I will set you free to worship and dwell with me* (see Ex. 3:1–15).

Centuries later still, David and Solomon built a temple in Jerusalem, and God filled it powerfully with his presence. For Israel, this was a new phase of God's promise being fulfilled: *I am your God, and you are my treasured people* (see 2 Chron. 7:1–22).

Across the Old Testament, God remained with his people, and they belonged to him, but something more was needed. God's people couldn't keep his laws and couldn't save themselves.

In sending his Son, God made a way for us to dwell with him forever. Jesus, the eternal Son of God, took on flesh and entered our darkness, loneliness, and hopelessness. He kept the law perfectly—thus fulfilling its righteous requirement. Throughout his earthly life, Jesus honored the Father and ministered to the poor and needy in the power and compassion of the Spirit. Yet his ultimate mission was one thing: to bear the penalty for our sins in dying on the cross. He lived the life we couldn't live and died the death that we deserved to die. Even his disciples fled from the cross at the moment of crucifixion. Most of all, Jesus suffered the worst possible loss: he bore the full wrath of God, forsaken according to his Father's plan (Matt. 27:46; Mark 15:34).

On the third day, though, the sun rose, the darkness fled, and the Son of God walked out of the grave. Jesus appeared to his disciples and friends, he shared a meal with them, and he promised to always be with them. The mission was complete. He came to set the captives free, to form a new family, to atone for our sins, and to make a way for us to return to God. He then ascended to heaven and gave his Holy Spirit to his followers. They were now full of his presence, and they would never be alone again.

Now, we who believe in Christ and turn from our sin are welcomed with open arms by the Father and filled with the Holy Spirit. Jesus suffered the greatest pain—being forsaken by the Father—so that we would never have to. He was thrust into darkness so that we could walk in the light. He was forsaken so that we could be included. *He suffered profound loneliness so that we could belong forever.*

So now the children of God belong to his family forever (John 8:35). In Christ, we form one body, and every member belongs to all the others (Rom. 12:5). We do good to all people, especially those who belong to the family of believers (Gal. 6:10). We cannot stop belonging to the body (1 Cor. 12:15–16). At the end of time, we will find ourselves among the diverse multitude, the ultimate and eternal place of belonging—the holy city (Rev. 21–22).

This is the message of the Scriptures: we belong to God, not ourselves or the world. Belonging to God means belonging to his family, the church.

Good News of Belonging

This biblical insight into how and where we belong brings us full circle. From the perspective of Scripture, *when we belong to God (not ourselves), we can then—and only then—fully belong to others.*

Indeed, only belonging to God—and through him, to one another in the church—can offer this secure position. Through repentance, we are forgiven of our sins. Through faith, we are joined to Christ in a vital, eternal union. When we believe, we are adopted into the family of God—made sons and daughters forever, heirs of the beautiful, eternal kingdom.

Belonging to God and his people means remarkable security in Christ. When we are secure in Christ, we will be established and rooted in how he has made us. In Christ, we can find true belonging. This, then, forms my definition for belonging: *True belonging is being fully known and fully loved—by God and by your community.*

Relational Beings

We can see the essential nature of human relationships in the earthly life and ministry of Jesus. He came into this world not from the heavens split wide open but by gently growing in his mother's womb. He came into a family, spent his childhood and early adulthood in obscurity, and then started his ministry by inviting others to follow him. Even on the eve of his crucifixion, he gathered for a meal with his disciples, then led them out to pray with him at Gethsemane. Among his final breaths, he instructed his disciples to care for his mother. On occasion, he left his disciples to pray in solitude—in order to cultivate his most important relationship, with his heavenly Father. But in general, Jesus did everything with this ragtag bunch of guys. His life and mission remind us that even he refused to live life in isolation. If relationships have always been essential to Jesus, shouldn't they be for us as well?

If Jesus was the most content and satisfied human ever, it shouldn't surprise us that a person cannot become fully whole without a community. A solitary life accepts burdens we were never made to carry.

The biblical story and our central message agree that we are created for community. This shouldn't surprise us, because it's God's nature to draw people into belonging. In Psalm 68, David praises our fatherly God:

> A father to the fatherless, a defender of widows,
>   is God in his holy dwelling.
> God sets the lonely in families,
>   he leads out the prisoners with singing;
>   but the rebellious live in a sun-scorched
>   land. (vv. 5–6 NIV)

What a beautiful phrase: He *"sets the lonely in families."* Loneliness is not a new condition, and God's redeeming work includes salvation from the deepest form of loneliness—isolation from God and his people.

Here, God is praised for being our Father, our defender, and our liberator. He leads us out of the prison of loneliness and into the freedom of family life: the eternal and global family of God. It is only in deep fellowship with God and this family that we can be most like Christ. And Christ is most glorified in us when our lives are marked by communion both with God and with each other.

The Hope of Spiritual Community

Do you know what the largest biological organism in the world is? I would have guessed the blue whale, and, well, I would have been wrong.

The largest known organism in the world is a network of aspen trees in Utah. This is what's unique about aspen trees: each "individual" tree is a part of a single, enormous root system. Above the surface, the aspens look like individual trees, each one reaching as high as a hundred feet. But beneath the surface, they're interconnected by a single root system. And the world's biggest organism? The Pando network of aspens spans 106 acres in Utah's Fishlake National Forest.[11]

This is a remarkable illustration for us. The Pando aspens are hundreds of thousands of trees, and each one will live up to 150 years. But they're all one organism, and the subterranean root system is believed to be eighty thousand years old. Each tree is unique and important, but it's completely supported by all the other aspens in the colony. Every tree has a vital role in the network during its time above the ground, but most deeply, the trees are one.[12]

Essentially, *that's what the church is.*

Above the surface, we are individual, unique, freestanding persons. Beneath the surface, we are interconnected by our root system, with all the branches leading back to a single root, which is Christ. As Jesus said: "Abide in me, and I in you. As the branch cannot bear fruit by itself, unless it abides in the vine, neither can you, unless you abide in me" (John 15:4). We are intimately and permanently connected to each other beneath the surface, rooted in Christ, with a single source of energy and life flowing through us—namely, the person of the Holy Spirit.

We are relational beings, designed in the image of our triune God. We've been created for life together, and apart from community, we'll never be fully whole and Christlike. In the church, we can resist the trends of social isolation and loneliness, discover our true home in Christ and his church, and find hope for a beautiful, deeply rooted community. We can finally belong.

So now the question becomes this: *How do we embody and practice this incredible truth—that we belong to God and one another?*

At the outset, I introduced three readers: a frustrated Christian on the fringes of the church, a local church pastor, and a committed church member and leader. As we consider how to cultivate deeper belonging together, I want to give practical help for each of these three readers.

Hope for the Lonely

For the frustrated, disaffected believer on the fringes of the church—feeling disconnected, unwanted, or not at the center of things—there's good news. True belonging is possible, and true, meaningful community can be cultivated. You can find a place to belong—to be fully known and fully loved by God and your community.

But like most worthwhile things, belonging won't come easy or without cost. What does it look like to discover (or rediscover) Christian community? I want to suggest three ways you can cultivate authentic community in your church: reset for relationships, take initiative in friendships, and find healing in relationships.

1. Reset for relationships. Since community doesn't come naturally, we have to reset many aspects of our lives. We have to slow down and resist the culture of hurry around us. It may mean that we're not able to work late into evenings or on weekends. Or it may mean we need concrete plans to attend weekly worship gatherings, to participate in a weekly small group or Bible study, or to serve with others in the community. A deep, connected life with others requires a new set of priorities and patterns. But it is worth it.

It's helpful to think of our daily lives in terms of discipleship patterns, the habits of life we have learned both intentionally and unintentionally. In this broad sense, discipleship is always happening: We become what we consume, as our patterns of life direct and dictate our deepest feelings, thoughts, and motives. We are always being conformed to the heart and personality and lifestyle of another person or system.

In *The Spirit of the Disciplines*, Dallas Willard wrote that the primary way we are conformed to Jesus (once we are regenerated, and united to him by faith) is by following him in the overall pattern of his earthly life.[13] With the help of the Holy Spirit, by obeying Jesus's teachings, meditating on his sufferings, death, and resurrection, and practicing his way of life, we become like him. It follows, then, that if the way to become like Christ is to follow his way of life, then Jesus's own earthly friendships should point us to the ideal pattern of human flourishing in relationships.

To do this, we need to repattern our lives around relationships—our fellowship with God and our fellowships with others. We cannot love others only in theory, saying we love others while hardly knowing them or spending time with them. We must prioritize the long obedience of relationship building, serving and caring for others even when it is most difficult for us.

2. Take the initiative in friendships. I've heard countless people over my years of ministry say that they don't feel connected or that people haven't reached out to them. I always begin by lamenting that with them. But I also remind them that those with the deepest connections are typically those who take the initiative.

Once again, the earthly life of Jesus provides an important pattern. Jesus frequently took initiative with others.

- He showed devotion to his closest friends, the disciples (Mark 3:13–19).
- He pursued disliked community members (Luke 5:29–32; 19:1–10).
- He engaged in conversation with those of other cultures (Luke 7:1–10; John 4:7–9).
- He ate with friends, family members, and guests (Luke 10:38–42; 11:37–38; 22:14–38).
- He attended weddings, funerals, and cultural events (Matt. 26:17–25; John 2:1–12).
- He pursued relationships with the poor and needy (Luke 7:36–50; see also 14:12–24).

Jesus's earthly life demonstrates a deep commitment to relationships and a remarkable sense of initiative. Further, he was never in a hurry, he embraced meals with others, and he accepted nearly every invitation that was made to him. Although his primary work was to proclaim the kingdom, call people to repentance and faith, and gather disciples to himself, Jesus hardly did anything alone. After all, his time on earth had a singular purpose: to glorify God by returning his lost sheep to him.

If this is how the Son of God ordered his life on this earth, what would it look like for us to follow in his ways? To not only play the host but join people where they are? To pursue those outside the fold? To attend gatherings and events with intentionality and for the sake of others' (and our) spiritual transformation?

For those in my own congregation who are feeling disconnected or on the fringes, I resist promising that others will soon reach out to them. I remind them that many others at church are new and trying to find their way as well. If you're waiting for someone to walk up to you and strike up conversation, there's a good chance they're waiting for you to do the same.

My experience has been that those who take initiative are the ones who have the most and deepest relationships in the church. It's a vitally important practice. Nonetheless, for those of us who have suffered church hurt, there's another step we must take.

3. *Find healing in relationships.* Many of my close friends who have left the church have suffered real disappointment and hurt at the hands of Christians. Some have suffered tragic spiritual abuse from ministry leaders.

It's no surprise, then, that they have moved away from Christian community. I mourn for my sisters and brothers who have gone looking for God and family only to find judgment, condemnation, and abuse.

Perhaps this is where you find yourself. If so, it's likely you feel torn between wanting to run as far from the church as possible and, at the same time, longing to return to it for healing and recovery. As I have pastored countless people (young and old) in this spot, my counsel is this: *since we are hurt in relationships, we can only find healing in relationships.*

When others sin against us, our natural tendency is to move away from all other people. When we sin ourselves—or merely disappoint others—it's natural to withdraw into shame and isolation. But while this withdrawal may be a natural survival instinct, it won't lead to our complete healing. At some point, we must move toward others to find comfort and healing. As relational beings, we can't learn to trust others, build friendships, or become whole through an isolated life.

If you are a child of God, you have been called and commissioned to live for him with purpose, dignity, and giftedness. Don't let those who have sinned against you determine your future. You may need to seek wise counseling and spiritual direction, and it may take time. But healing and renewal can be found in Christ and his church. You can move toward others with trust and hope again, not because your next community won't fail you *but because God will never fail you*. And the Lord often ministers to us through the presence and love of others.

Dear friend, hurt and frustrated by the church, I want to lovingly encourage you: Don't give up. Hang in there. Seek the Lord with others, and recommit to life in an imperfect church community.[14]

Hope for Pastors and Church Leaders

Next, I want to offer hope, encouragement, and wisdom to pastors and other vocational church leaders. We sure do have a hard job! And of all the many things we do, cultivating spiritual community in a lonely world ranks among the most difficult, time-consuming, and personally demanding efforts. But once again, I want to encourage you: it is worth it, for you and your churches.

1. Take the initiative. I already suggested this step for the believer on the fringes, but it's just as important for pastors too! It can be difficult for a pastor to build and maintain genuine personal relationships in the church. Your church may want you to remain a distinct, distant professional, offering your expertise without being personally connected to their lives. But this aloofness is to be resisted. For your own sake, for your family's health, and for your church's growth, take the initiative in forming deep relationships in your local church body.

While you should also maintain key friendships and relationships outside your local church, let your church be your primary community as you also seek growth in Christ as a relational being. How? Join or lead a small group. Rather than meeting only with leaders, connect with a regular fellowship group, and even if you lead, make clear that you are still an ordinary and needy Christian. Invite people to spend time together: although church leaders meet with people for a living, consider having two or three meetings or gatherings (coffee, lunch, or evening get-togethers) each week for the sole purpose of building relationships. Form and maintain two or three deep relationships: Jesus had Peter, James, and John; similarly, we would do well to have a few close friends in our own church communities with whom we can be completely present, honest, and trusting.

Involve other families in your family's activities: if you are married with kids, find ways to invite other families to the things you're already doing—go to the park together, invite others to your own kids' activities, and welcome other families to your weekend and holiday get-togethers.

2. Model the way. Paul told Timothy, "Set the believers an example in speech, in conduct, in love, in faith, in purity" (1 Tim. 4:12). He also told Titus, "Show yourself in all respects to be a model of good works" (Titus 2:7). While Paul was primarily encouraging these young pastors in their teaching and moral purity, the principle holds for all areas of leaders' lives. The church watches you, and they are likely to model much of their spiritual and relational habits after yours. Thus, show them the way of relational depth and interdependence.

There are a few practical ways that you can model Christ-shaped relationships. I encourage pastors to regularly use sermon illustrations from their community group or friendships in the church—with permission when necessary. Further, when meeting with new people in the church, tell them about the community you have found, and urge them to follow the steps that have most helped you. For those struggling to make friends and build relationships, share how you've struggled in the same way but persevered to create a close-knit community. For those with families, share how you have involved other families in your children's activities. Model the way of friendship and community, and others will be glad to follow the pattern.

3. *Focus on simple, sustainable ministry.* If you're like me, you likely work long days and full weeks and have little spare time to invest in new friendships and other families. (This is part of why it's so helpful to invite others to things you're already doing.) To embrace a life of relationships, we will have to be more intentional in how we structure our churches' ministries. We will have to focus on simple, sustainable ministry instead of running too many events and unwieldy programs.

It's natural for church members to want to meet felt needs and provide numerous connection points—especially when wanting to cultivate deeper community. But we must be careful. If we say yes to every new group, class, service opportunity, and ministry event, we will soon have a church calendar so full that it's almost impossible to build relationships outside of structured church events. Plus, each of these events demands more time in preparation and administration for volunteer leaders, limiting their capacity to develop deep friendships.

I'll be honest: I love ending events and programs that have reached their expiration date. Early in my ministry, I was so afraid of disappointing or offending people that I would let studies, groups, and recurring events go on forever. But after seeing the value of free time for friendship and community, I've grown to appreciate saying no to new things and graciously ending things that have fulfilled their purpose so that members have free time to build relationships together.

I'll give one simple example. When we first began planting Trinity Church, we thought offering free family movies in the park would be a great way to connect with our neighborhood. It was a great idea, but the volunteer need was immense. We bought a large, inflatable screen and borrowed a projector and sound system. We canvassed the neighborhood with invitations, secured park reservations, obtained movie licenses, and posted on social media. We set up the event, transported and stored the items, and cleaned up afterward. It was exhausting. And in the year that we held these move nights, we spent thousands of volunteer hours, and not a single person from the neighborhood ever visited the church. Gaining church attendees wasn't our only goal, but it had become clear that this ministry was not bearing the fruit we desired. So we ended it. And nearly everyone breathed a sigh of relief. (Now, we make the projector, screen, and sound system available to any community groups that want to throw their own neighborhood party.)

Pastor, you have an incredibly difficult and demanding position. You have been called to teach the word, pray with and for your people, and shepherd the flock under the care of the good shepherd. But don't neglect your own life and relationships, and don't forget to lead the church in forming and sustaining healthy, deep relationships. I'm convinced you won't regret guarding these priorities.

How Every Member Can Cultivate Community

Finally, I want to consider my third reader—the committed believer, church member, and volunteer leader.

1. Practice hospitality. Hospitality is the distinctively Christian practice of creating space for others. It is not just opening our homes; it's the Christlike pattern of opening our hearts and lives as well. Hospitality, in a biblical sense, includes creating space in our homes for our brothers and sisters in Christ, creating space in our schedules and hearts for those who don't know the Lord, creating space in our community groups for our neighbors and coworkers, and creating space in our lives for the poor and marginalized.

Just as Christ came to us when we were outsiders, so the church can open its heart and doors to those who don't know him. In Paul's instructions for the church to embrace self-giving love for each other, he includes a strong exhortation to "show hospitality" (Rom. 12:13). And while Paul's exhortation is aimed at hospitality within the church, hospitality is also a missional practice in a lonely world. As one Christian author put it:

> In our world full of strangers, estranged from their own past, culture and country, from their neighbors, friends and family, from their deepest self and their God, we witness a painful search for a hospitable place where life can be lived without fear and where community can be found. . . . That

is our vocation [as Christians]: to convert the . . .
enemy into the guest and to create the free and
fearless space where brotherhood and sisterhood
can be formed and fully experienced.[15]

Let's pause now and consider our own stories. At one
point, we were all visitors to a church and didn't know
more than a person or two. How might our lives be different at this point if no one had invited us in and given
us a place at the table?

Every one of us has been the recipient of the hospitality of others, and now we extend that same hospitable
spirit to the next generation of church visitors—and to
our own neighbors, coworkers, and friends. This vision
of hospitality is more than mere entertaining, of course.
Entertaining includes setting out our best food, showing
off our homes, and inviting our most attractive guests;
it puts the focus on us. (Remember, Jesus didn't own a
home, and yet he is our model of hospitality.)

Biblical hospitality puts the focus on others. We are
making space for them to experience friendship and
belonging. We can invite disconnected believers into
our homes as an expression of the love of the church.

We can serve and bless the single mother in our congregation by encouraging her to drop off her kids for a few hours. We can bring a meal and sit with the older member who lives in an assisted living facility. We can invite the unbelieving friend or family over for dinner and ask intentional questions about their relationships, beliefs, fears, and hopes. Our vocation as Christians is to create space for others, demonstrating the welcoming embrace of Jesus himself.[16]

2. Pray together. This may seem simple, even assumed, but to cultivate true Christian community, we will be wise to prioritize prayer together. If we are to be a truly *spiritual* community and not just another social club or friend clique, we must pursue and enjoy God's presence together. In the past two decades, nearly every Christian book on community I've read has used the phrase "do life together." I've said countless times, "It's not enough to just go to church and community group; we can and should be *doing life together*." And I do believe that. But I also believe that "doing life together" is not enough. Anyone can "do life together" and be unchanged by it—still just as impatient, unfriendly, greedy, or angry as before. Our goal as Christians is to glorify God through our conformity to Christ, to be gradually formed toward his character, love for others, and way of life. Thus, our relationships can and should do *spiritual* life together.

In my own congregation, we prioritize community groups and encourage folks to gather with their group members both regularly and spontaneously. We also encourage them to ask each other intentional questions, to pray for each other between gatherings and meetups, to care for each other through the challenges and crises of life. And we also encourage (and train) them to pray together, whether in formal group gatherings or informal times. It might seem odd at first to be talking to a friend and stop and say, "Can I pray with you right now?" But I can guarantee you: very rarely will someone say no, and very rarely will you regret taking a few moments to pray with a friend.

When we pray together as believers, we are doing far more than just supporting one another; we are connecting with the Father together. We are strengthening one another in faith and hope as we seek him as one. We are seeking the presence and power of Christ for the challenges of advancing his kingdom in a lonely world.

When we pray together, we know that Christ is with us (Matt. 18:20), making us more like him through the Spirit (2 Cor. 3:18).

3. *Stay present.* One of the sneaky challenges in our current age is transience. If we are moving to a new city every few years, it will be almost impossible to develop and maintain deep relationships. Similarly, if we stay in the same city but often change church communities, the same loss is likely.

Early church scholar Joseph Hellerman puts it well in *When the Church Was a Family*:

> Spiritual formation occurs primarily in the context of community. People who remain connected with their brothers and sisters in the local church almost invariably grow in self-understanding, and they mature in their ability to relate in healthy ways to God and to their fellow human beings. This is especially the case for those courageous Christians who stick it out through the often messy process of interpersonal discord and conflict resolution. Long-term

interpersonal relationships are the crucible of genuine progress in the Christian life. People who stay grow.[17]

Indeed, I have found this observation to be remarkably true: *those who stay grow*. Sure, it will be harder and require seasons of patience and struggle. It may involve working through conflict with friends and others in your community. It might even mean passing up a promotion or raise that would require a move or longer hours. But it will be worth it in the long run.

Stability is one of the most important elements in a growing, thriving spiritual life. The most important formation we experience occurs over a long period of time. No one becomes like Jesus overnight. God typically works through a slow process, transforming his people in the everyday moments of life as we seek to follow him with all our hearts, souls, minds, and strength.

My most important and fulfilling relationships—the ones that really challenge and encourage me toward communion with God and growth in Christ—tend to be those I've had for five, ten, or twenty years. Many of these are with folks who have not been natural friends, and with some I've had significant conflict. But we've stayed together, and the longevity of our relationships has allowed us to see Christ's work in each other. Perhaps the main reason people don't experience deep, encouraging friendship more commonly is that they leave or move the year before it happens. Relationships take time, Christ-centered friendship is slow work, and stability is one of the most important things you can cultivate.

The Blessing of Belonging

These are simple steps, but, admittedly, they are difficult to take—and keep taking. It's easy to become discouraged. Our cynical world trains us not to expect much. And our hopes for friendships and community have been diminished by our own past negative experiences. But the church is *the* place where we experience and magnify Christ together. We may not have much in common besides Christ, and that in itself is a witness to the watching world. There is nothing more powerful and unifying and edifying than Christ-centered community. That's why so much of Paul's letters emphasize establishing healthy community in the local church through sacrificial relationships. It is possible, he believes, but it will require sacrifice, endurance, and devotion.

But what else would we give our lives to?

God has created us for relationship—to himself and to one another in the church. He has designed us as relational beings, with an inherent desire to connect and a need to belong. He has invited us to himself, promising to be our God and to give us a safe place to dwell now and forever. Jesus has come into our world, shattering the darkness, bearing rejection and loneliness on our behalf, and setting us free to receive lives of connection and fellowship. The Holy Spirit now fills our hearts and lives, bearing witness to the beauty and glory of Christ, and strengthening our relationships for unity together. And one day all evil and brokenness will become a distant memory. Heaven and earth will join as one, the believing dead will be raised physically, and we will live forever in the fullness of God's presence as a new city, a new family. Every tear will be wiped away, and every wound will be healed. We will belong to God and one another, without a single disruption or challenge, forever and ever.

This is our future, but we can move toward it now too. We have forgiveness of sins and union with Christ. We are loved by God the Father. We have the power and presence of the Spirit. And we are joined to one another as brothers and sisters in Christ. We gather for worship, prayer, communion, teaching, and fellowship. We open our homes and lives to one another. We help one another through the hardships and sufferings of life. We carry each other's burdens and uphold each other. And our love for each other is the greatest witness to the unbelieving world around us; our unity shines in a divided world.

Will it be easy? Of course not. Will it be worth it? Absolutely.

We are God's children. We are fully known and fully loved by him. We can be fully known and fully loved within his treasured possession, the church. We can belong.

Therefore, may we together embody the call of Romans 12:9–13:

> Let love be genuine. . . . Love one another with brotherly affection. Outdo one another in show-ing honor. Do not be slothful in zeal, be fervent in

44

spirit, serve the Lord. Rejoice in hope, be patient in tribulation, be constant in prayer. Contribute to the needs of the saints and seek to show hospitality.

Amen and amen.

Notes

1. See Jena McGregor, "This Surgeon General Says There's a 'Loneliness Epidemic,'" *Washington Post*, October 4, 2017, https://www.washingtonpost.com/; Jane E. Brody, "The Surprising Effects of Loneliness on Health," *New York Times*, December 11, 2017, https://www.nytimes.com/; Jayne O'Donnell and Shari Rudavsky, "Young Americans Are the Loneliest, Surprising Study from Cigna Shows," *USA Today*, May 1, 2018, https://www.usatoday.com/; Olga Khazon, "How Loneliness Begets Loneliness," *Atlantic*, April 6, 2017, https://www.theatlantic.com/; Dhruv Khullar, "How Social Isolation Is Killing Us," *New York Times*, December 22, 2016, https://www.nytimes.com/.
2. Vivek Murthy, "Work and the Loneliness Epidemic," *Harvard Business Review*, September 26, 2017, https://hbr.org/.

3. Julianne Holt-Lunstad, Timothy B. Smith, and J. Bradley Layton, "Social Relationships and Mortality Risk: A Meta-analytic Review," *PLOS Med* 7, no. 7 (2010), https://doi.org/10.1371/journal.pmed.1000316.

4. Robert D. Putnam, *Bowling Alone: The Collapse and Revival of American Community* (New York: Simon and Schuster, 2001).

5. Marc J. Dunkelman, *The Vanishing Neighbor: The Transformation of American Community* (New York: Norton, 2014), xvii.

6. Ben Casselman and Ella Koeze, "The Pandemic Changed How We Spent Our Time," *New York Times*, July 27, 2021, https://www.nytimes.com/.

7. David French, "Lost Friendships Break Hearts and Nations," *Dispatch*, July 11, 2021, https://frenchpress.the dispatch.com/.

8. Tim Keller, "Social Media, Identity, and the Church," *Life in the Gospel*, Summer 2021, https://quarterly.gospel inlife.com/social-media-identity-and-the-church/.

9. Roy F. Baumeister and Mark R. Leary, "The Need to Belong: Desire for Interpersonal Attachments as Fundamental Human Motivation," *Psychological Bulletin* 117, no. 3 (1995), https://psycnet.apa.org/.

10. Baumeister and Leary, "The Need to Belong."

11. Arthur C. Brooks, *From Strength to Strength: Finding Success, Happiness, and Deep Purpose in the Second Half of Life* (New York: Portfolio, 2022), 112.

12. "Quaking Aspen," National Park Service, February 1, 2023, https://www.nps.gov/brca/learn/nature/quaking aspen.htm.

13. Dallas Willard, *The Spirit of the Disciplines: Understanding How God Changes Lives* (San Francisco: HarperOne, 1999), ix.

14. For more on this theme, see Jeremy Linneman, "Embrace True Belonging in the Church," in *Before You Lose Your Faith: Deconstructing Doubt in the Church*, ed. Ivan Mesa (Wheaton, IL: Gospel Coalition, 2021).

15. Henri J. M. Nouwen, *Reaching Out: Three Movements of the Spiritual Life* (New York: Image, 1986), 65–66.

16. I write more about this in my short book *Life-Giving Groups: How to Grow Healthy, Multiplying Community Groups* (Louisville: Sojourn Network, 2018).

17. Joseph H. Hellerman, *When the Church Was a Family: Recapturing Jesus' Vision for Authentic Christian Community* (Nashville: B&H Academic, 2009), 1.

Recommended Resources

Butterfield, Rosaria. *The Gospel Comes with a House Key: Practicing Radically Ordinary Hospitality in Our Post-Christian World*. Wheaton, IL: Crossway, 2018. This important book provides a blueprint for hospitality and ordinary community in local churches.

Chester, Tim. *A Meal with Jesus: Discovering Grace, Community, and Mission around the Table*. Wheaton, IL: Crossway, 2011. Chester's book is a practical, compelling guide to hospitality "around the table." He shows how Jesus's meals form a significant aspect of his ministry and how our hospitality today offers those inside and outside the church a space to discover and grow in Christ.

Hellerman, Joseph H. *When the Church Was a Family: Recovering Jesus' Vision for Authentic Christian Community*.

Nashville: B&H Academic, 2009. This is my favorite book on the relational dynamics of the early church.

Ince, Irwyn L., Jr. *Beautiful Community: Unity, Diversity, and the Church at Its Best*. Downers Grove, IL: InterVarsity Press, 2020. Ince offers a hopeful, biblical foundation for multiethnic churches.

Keller, Timothy. *Center Church: Doing Balanced, Gospel-Centered Ministry in Your City*. Grand Rapids, MI: Zondervan, 2012. This has been the most important book for our church-planting ministry. The chapters on gospel renewal, missional community, and integrative ministry will be especially helpful for cultivating deep community in your church.

Linneman, Jeremy. *Life-Giving Groups: How to Grow Healthy, Multiplying Community Groups*. Louisville: Sojourn Network, 2018. I wrote this short book for our family of churches, now called Harbor Network. I focus on the practical elements of spiritual formation, hospitality, and mission in community and also provide a more comprehensive list of resources on small groups and community.

McKnight, Scot. *A Fellowship of Differents: Showing the World God's Design for Life Together*. Grand Rapids, MI:

Zondervan, 2016. McKnight makes a compelling case for how the church is strengthened by diversity in its communities. He also provides helpful application for local church communities.

Nouwen, Henri J. M. *Reaching Out: Three Movements of the Spiritual Life*. New York: Image, 1986. This small book contains a section on hospitality that is my favorite work on the topic. Nouwen was a Catholic spiritual writer, so I don't agree with all of his theology, but he has been one of my favorite authors for many years.

Scripture Index

TGC | THE GOSPEL COALITION

The Gospel Coalition (TGC) supports the church in making disciples of all nations, by providing gospel-centered resources that are trusted and timely, winsome and wise.

Guided by a Council of more than 40 pastors in the Reformed tradition, TGC seeks to advance gospel-centered ministry for the next generation by producing content (including articles, podcasts, videos, courses, and books) and convening leaders (including conferences, virtual events, training, and regional chapters).

In all of this we want to help Christians around the world better grasp the gospel of Jesus Christ and apply it to all of life in the 21st century. We want to offer biblical truth in an era of great confusion. We want to offer gospel-centered hope for the searching.

Join us by visiting TGC.org so you can be equipped to love God with all your heart, soul, mind, and strength, and to love your neighbor as yourself.

TGC.org

TGC Hard Questions Series

Does God Care about Gender Identity?
Samuel D. Ferguson

Is Christianity Good for the World?
Sharon James

Why Do We Feel Lonely at Church?
Jeremy Linneman

TGC Hard Questions is a series of short booklets that seek to answer common but difficult questions people ask about Christianity. The series serves the church by providing tools that answer unchurched people's deep longings for community, their concerns about biblical ethics, and their doubts about confessional faith.

For more information, visit **crossway.org**.

Also Available from the Gospel Coalition

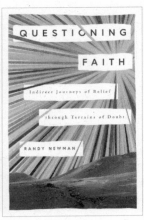

For more information, visit **crossway.org**.